HYDROPONIC BASICS

by George F. Van Patten

**I would like to thank the countless gardeners and hydroponic merchants that provided valuable input and support to make this book possible.
Thank you all! Special thanks from me and from all the hydroponic enthusiasts that read this book!**

Published in the United States of America
Copyright 2004 by George F. Van Patten
9 8 7 6 5 4 3 2 1
ISBN: 1-878823-25-6

Editor: Estella Cervantes
Layouts and Design: J. Chris Thompson
Artwork: J. Chris Thompson & Peio
Typesetting: J. Chris Thompson and ASR Graphics (UK) +44 (0) 23 9283 0581
Photos: George F. Van Patten, and the stores listed below.
Cover Photos: George F. Van Patten and Sunny Bueck

We want to give a special thanks to Sunny Bueck and all the hydroponic stores and manufacturers that contributed photos to this book.

Alternative Garden Supply, Chicago, IL
Albuquerque (AHL) Hydroponics, Albuquerque, NM
American Hydroponics, Arcata, CA
Green Air Products, Gresham, OR
General Hydroponics, Sebastapol, CA
General Hydroponics, Europe
Guala Robotics, Denver, CO
Hydroculture Guy Dionne, Montreal, PQ
Hydrofarm, Petaluma, CA
L'Interior, Barcelona, Spain
Nature's Control, Medford, OR
Rambridge, Calgary, AB
Sunlite Supply, Vancouver, WA
Sure Growth, Delta, BC
Terraponic, Vancouver, BC
The Plant, Barcelona, Spain
Worm's Way, Bloomington, IN

Table of Contents

We Need Your Photos!

We are working on new, 100 percent color, gardening books. Would you like to see your garden photographs featured in our books? Here is how you can do it!

- We need high resolution and high quality digital photos of indoor hydroponic gardens and greenhouses with the parameters that follow:
- Your camera must record images at three mega pixels or more.
- Digital files should be a minimum of one megabyte in a .JPG or TIF format.
- Images should be well lighted.
- Images should be in focus.
- If possible, photograph your garden from beginning to end.
- The more images we have to choose from, the better the chances of your photos appearing in our books.

Have fun!

Please send questions and low resolution images for consideration to us at vanpatten@gardeningindoors.com

Here are examples of three bad photos and one good photo.

◀ Bad - out of focus

▶ Bad - flat, lacks contrast and too dark. No flash used.

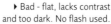

◀ Bad - in focus, bad angle and a little too much light from flash.

▶ Good, in focus and good lighting. Shot with flash. Could reduce flash a little.

CHAPTER ONE

WHY HYDROPONICS?

Hydroponics is a simple, easy way to grow plants. Hydroponics is superior to growing in soil because you can give plants maximum levels of the exact nutrients they need. Precise control of nutrient uptake makes it possible to reap higher yields faster.

◄ High Intensity Discharge (HID) lamps bring the sunshine indoors. If you are unable to use natural sunlight, HIDs allow the gardener to control the hours of light per day as well as spectrum and intensity.

◄ A vent or extraction fan is required to change depleted and stale air for fresh, new air that is packed with carbon dioxide (CO_2), the stuff that plants need to grow.

▶ An accurate maximum-minimum thermometer and hygrometer are indispensable in a garden room. Plants grow poorly above 75° F and below 55° F. The ideal relative humidity for different plants ranges from 30% to 70% or more. Precise control of temperature and humidity are essential to rapid, healthy growth.

◄ An oscillating-circulation fan is vital to keep air from stratifying in garden rooms. Plants use all of the CO_2 around the leaves quickly. This air must be replaced with new, fresh CO_2-rich air.

Hydroponic systems are simple, easy to use, and understand. All the parts on this ebb-and-flow system are labeled.

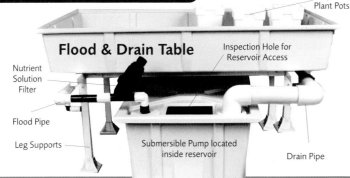

Flood & Drain Table

Square Plant Pots

Inspection Hole for Reservoir Access

Nutrient Solution Filter

Flood Pipe

Leg Supports

Submersible Pump located inside reservoir

Drain Pipe

How A Plant Works

Leaves are where photosynthesis – the process in which sunlight combines with CO_2 and water and is then taken up by the roots to manufacture food (carbohydrates) for the plant – takes place and oxygen is released as a by-product. Plants regulate small openings, stomata, on leaf undersides to allow CO_2 to enter and oxygen (O_2) to exit. When open, stomata allow water vapor to escape in the process of transpiration.

Roots anchor a plant in the ground and absorb water, nutrients, and air. Hydroponics allows absorption of water, nutrients, and air at an accelerated rate. Tiny root hairs increase the surface area for absorption. These root hairs are very delicate and must be moist at all times. Large roots are similar to stems. They transport water and dissolved minerals (fertilizer) in the phloem.

Stems have a vascular system to transport water and nutrients throughout the plant. The *xylem* carries water and dissolved minerals from roots to leaves. The *phloem* transports food manufactured by leaves to the stems and roots. The vascular cambium is the growth zone that produces xylem on one side and phloem on the other. The stem also supports the plant and bears leaves, buds, flowers, and fruit.

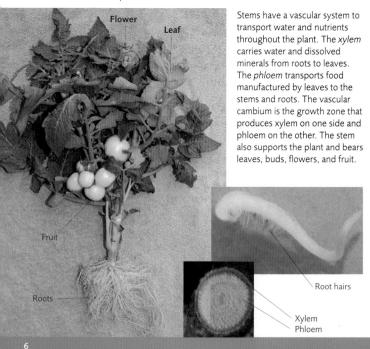

Flower

Leaf

Fruit

Roots

Root hairs

Xylem
Phloem

CHAPTER TWO

ATMOSPHERE

Plants have five basic needs. Each one accounts for 20 percent of a plant's ability to grow to its maximum potential. When all of these needs are met at the maximum potential, the result is maximum growth (20% x 5 = 100%). If one of the needs arrives at only 15 percent, all growth is impaired equally (15% x 5 = 75%). If two or more of the basic needs are not met, growth slows quickly. Even with the best hydroponic system money can buy, in a garden where relative-air humidity is 80 percent when it should be 50 percent, growth will be limited. The dollars and high hopes invested in a hydroponic system can easily be 'dashed' in a cloud of hot, humid air.

Air   20%

- Temperature
- Humidity
- CO_2 and O_2 content

Light   20%

- Spectrum (color)
- Intensity
- Photoperiod (hours of light per day)

Water   20%

- Temperature
- pH
- EC
- Oxygen content

Nutrients   20%

- Composition
- Purity

Growing Medium   20%

- Air content
- Moisture content

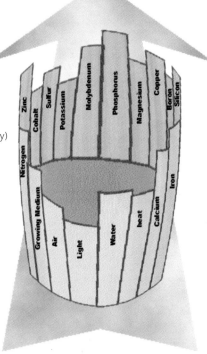

VENTILATION AND CIRCULATION

▲ Vent or exhaust fans remove hot, humid, and depleted air from the garden area. They are available in three basic types each with advantages and disadvantages.

The propeller on an in-line extraction fan is similar to that of a jet airplane. These fans use principles from both muffin fans and squirrel cage blowers. They move air from one side to the other quickly, quietly, and efficiently.

◄ The muffin fan, with propeller-like blades, requires a large opening to move air through. When rotating slowly, a large volume of air is extracted from the garden room with minimum noise.

◄ Squirrel cage blowers move large quantities of air through a small outlet or ducting. They move a lot of air for their size, but create noise in the process.

▼ Flexible ducting is easier to use than rigid ducting. To install, run the duct the shortest distance possible and cut curves to a minimum. When turned at more than 30 degrees, much of the air that enters a duct will not exit the other end. Keep the ducting straight and short!

30° up to 20% loss of air transmission

45° up to 40% loss of air transmission

90° up to 60% loss of air transmission

Hot air rises and cool air sinks. To evacuate hot, humid air, always install vent fans as high as possible in the garden room.

Gardeners often install a fresh air intake fan in garden rooms. Install an intake fan the same size as the exhaust fan for the best airflow.

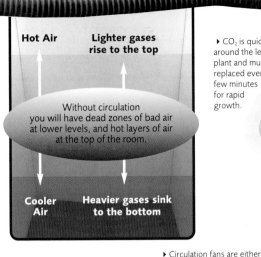

Hot Air **Lighter gases rise to the top**

Without circulation you will have dead zones of bad air at lower levels, and hot layers of air at the top of the room.

Cooler Air **Heavier gases sink to the bottom**

▶ CO_2 is quickly used around the leaves of a plant and must be replaced every few minutes for rapid growth.

CO_2 rich air layer
CO_2 poor air layer

▶ Circulation fans are either fixed or oscillating. Fixed or stationary fans blow air in a single direction. If trained directly on a few plants, excessive air will dry them out quickly while other plants do not receive enough air.

▼ Oscillating fans move air in a wide radius. Some oscillating fans physically move back and forth. Set them on a table or mount them on a wall or ceiling.

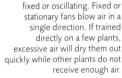

▶ In another type of circulation fan, a rotating-louvered panel moves to oscillate air around the room. This type of fan can be set on the floor, table, or mounted on the ceiling.

Train circulation fans, so they make leaves flutter, to enhance air circulation immediately around plants. Air circulation keeps warm and cool air mixed together. Oscillating fans can also be trained to blow hot air up toward the vent fan.

TEMPERATURE AND HUMIDITY

Relative humidity climbs quickly when temperatures fall at night. Conversely, the same amount of water (humidity) is still in the air when the temperature rises. Take maximum-minimum readings every day and night, and plot the findings on graph paper for a partial overview of the climate in the garden room.

◄ An accurate thermometer is an absolute 'must' in the garden. You will need the thermometer to check the ambient-air temperature both day and night, and the temperature of the nutrient solution in the reservoir.

◄ 50% Relative Humidity is ideal for most gardens.

◄ A digital maximum-minimum thermometer/ hygrometer makes monitoring the temperature and humidity as easy as pressing a button.

A 10 x 10 x 8 foot (800 cubic feet) garden room can hold:

4 oz. of water at 32 degrees F.
7 oz. of water at 50 degrees F.
14 oz. of water at 70 degrees F.
18 oz. of water at 80 degrees F.
28 oz. of water at 90 degrees F.
56 oz. of water at 100 degrees F.

▲ A combination thermometer-hygrometer makes checking temperature and humidity quick and easy.

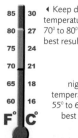

◄ Keep daytime temperature at 70° to 80° F for best results.

▶ Keep night-time temperature at 55° to 60° F for best results.

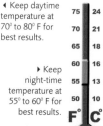

▶ Keep nutrient solution at 55° to 60° F for best results.

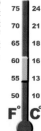

ATMOSPHERIC CONTOLLERS

◀ A thermostat is attached to the vent fan. The thermostat is set at 75° F. The thermostat will turn on the vent fan when the temperature rises above 75° F.

A humidistat is also attached to the vent fan. The humidistat is set, both day and night, at 70 percent when plants are in vegetative growth and 50 percent when flowering. The vent fan is activated when humidity rises above the desired level.

◀ Humidistats are available from many different manufacturers. They are designed to withstand the demanding conditions in a garden room and are very convenient and easy to use.

◀ Sophisticated controllers manage several different devices: vent fans, heaters, air conditioning, and CO_2 disbursement. Some controllers are equipped with remote sensors and computer interfaces.

LIGHTING

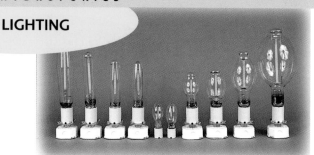

▲ **High intensity discharge (HID) lamps** used for growing plants are either a high-pressure (HP) sodium lamp, which emits a bright, yellowish light; or metal halide, which emits white light similar to natural sunlight. Bulbs are either tubular or bulbous and require a special socket, ballast, and capacitor. Some HP sodium bulbs require a starter. Popular lamps for gardening include: 150, 175, 250, 270, 400, 430, 600, 1000, and 1100 wattages.

▲ **Fluorescent lamps** are perfect for growing low-light plants, seedlings, and cuttings. Plants, including seedlings and cuttings, grow best under lamps with a spectrum similar to natural sunlight. Flowering plants benefit from more reddish-yellow light. The most popular fluorescent bulbs are 20 and 40 watts and are available in T-8, T-10, and T-12 sizes; the smaller the number, the brighter the bulb.

◀ **Compact fluorescent light bulbs** are bright and efficient. They can be used to grow both high- and low-light plants. They are available from 7 to 200 watts. The larger bulbs, 55-, 65-, 95-, 125-, and 200-watt bulbs are acceptable to grow high-light plants.

▶ The European 55 watt compact-fluorescent lamps are 50 centimeters (about 20 inches) long.

Reflective hoods come in all shapes and sizes. Buy a reflective hood that disperses light evenly over the garden. Avoid reflectors with a mirror finish and creases in the construction. Horizontal bulb orientation is more efficient than vertical orientation.

▲ The versatile Adjust-A-Wing reflects bright light efficiently and evenly over gardens.

▲ Many reflective hoods use dual-parabolic arches contained by an outer hood. This reflective hood also uses a pebble-pounded reflective metal.

▲ Parabolic domes employ a less efficient vertical-lamp orientation. Such reflective hoods can be placed close to the garden canopy. They are ideal for plants requiring less light.

◀ Use a light meter to measure the amount of light a reflector throws. This meter will save you much wasted light when purchasing and employing a reflector.

▲ A light-mover trolleys lamps back and forth over the garden. Moving lamps create less heat and distributes light more evenly over the plants. The lamp can be placed closer to the plants, increasing efficiency.

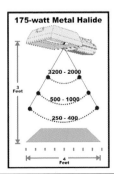

175-watt Metal Halide

3 Feet

3200 - 2000

500 - 1000

250 - 400

4 Feet

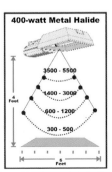

400-watt Metal Halide

4 Feet

3500 - 5500

1400 - 3000

600 - 1200

300 - 500

6 Feet

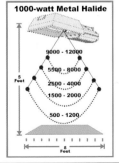

1000-watt Metal Halide

5 Feet

9000 - 12000

5500 - 8000

2500 - 4000

1500 - 2000

500 - 1200

8 Feet

ELECTRICITY

Watts   Amps   Volts

Whether gardening indoors, in a greenhouse, or outdoors, you will need electricity.

As you know, electricity and water don't mix.

  Watt is a measure of work.

  Ampere (amp) is a measure of electricity in motion.

Volt is a measure of electricity under pressure.

Ground fault interrupter (GFI) outlets add an extra element of safety. The breaker switch in the GFI outlet turns off the electricity when the circuit is overloaded. Use a GFI in all garden rooms.

◀ A breaker switch will 'trip' or turn off when the electrical circuit is overloaded.

▼ White and black wires conduct electricity. The green ground wire is for safety.

OHMS POWER LAW: VOLTS X AMPERES = WATTS
110 VOLTS X 3.6 AMPS = 396 WATTS
220 VOLTS X 1.8 AMPS = 396 WATTS

Getting shocked is no fun and it can kill you! A simple rule to follow: keep electrical insulations above the belt line and water below the belt line.

Circuits in breaker boxes are rated in amperes. If you assume North American electricity standards of 115-volts you can follow the chart below to find the number of amperes each circuit will tolerate.

OVERLOAD CHART

Ampere Rating	Amperes Available	Amperes Overload
15	13	14
20	16	17
25	20	21
30	24	25
40	32	33

INNOVATIVE MANUFACTURERS HAVE DEVELOPED
SOPHISTICATED TIMERS TO PERFORM COMPLEX FUNCTIONS.

Timers keep the garden on schedule. You will need a timer to turn lights on and off. Many hydroponic systems require a timer to control the irrigation schedule of the garden.

The ballast regulates electricity with a transformer and capacitor to operate the HID lamp. Some HP sodium lamps require a separate starter. An outer box protects the internal components from water and the gardener. The ballast is connected to a timer.

▲ Heavy-duty timers can control several HID lamps.

◄ A 15-ampere, 115-volt digital timer is used for a 1000-watt lamp.

▸ Pins in this simple dial timer can be set to turn hydroponic systems on/off several times a day.

▾ Dual Timers offer flexibility.

COST OF ELECTRICITY CHART

Cost per KWH	12-hour days day	month	18-hour days day	month
$0.05	0.60	18.00	0.90	27.00
$0.06	0.72	21.60	1.08	32.40
$0.07	0.84	25.20	1.26	37.80
$0.08	0.96	28.80	1.44	43.20
$0.09	1.08	32.40	1.62	48.60
$0.10	1.20	36.00	1.80	54.00
$0.15	1.80	54.00	2.70	81.00
$0.20	2.40	72.00	3.60	108.00
$0.25	3.00	90.00	4.50	135.00

POLLEN AND FRAGRANCE

Some people are allergic to pollen, plants, and odors. This condition can be debilitating. Avoid such problems with charcoal filters and ozone generators. Masking agents are also available, if fragrances are annoying.

▸ Generator fits in the garden room. It releases ozone into the air which mixes with the air. Always follow manufacturer's instructions, and do not look at the UV bulb, as it is harmful to the eyes.

◂ An ozone generator is installed into ducting, so vented air can be treated with ozone. The O_3 must mix with O_2 for a minute or longer in order to neutralize fragrances before being expelled outside.

▸ Charcoal filters clean the air. The model shown has a half-inch outer filter that encases porous ducting and is surrounded by activated charcoal. These filters are efficient until humidity climbs beyond 60 percent; at this point moisture-filled charcoal fails to absorb properly.

◂ Some gardeners prefer to use essential oils to overpower or enhance the fragrance. These products are available in liquid, gel, and spray forms.

Ozone generators convert oxygen (O_2) into ozone (O_3) by exposing the air to ultraviolet (UV) light. The extra oxygen molecule in ozone attaches to particles' negating fragrance. Once the molecule is shed, O_3 is converted back into O_2.

Ozone generators are rated in the number of cubic feet they are able to treat. Figure cubic feet by multiplying the length x width x height of the room.

CARBON DIOXIDE

Carbon dioxide (CO_2) is a colorless, odorless, non-flammable gas in the air that occurs at the rate of 0.035 to 0.04 percent. Rapidly growing plants can use up to 0.15 percent (1500 PPM). When given more CO_2, many plants grow faster and bigger. Growth slows dramatically when the CO_2 level falls below 0.02 percent.

◀ CO_2 emitters contain a regulator, flow meter, and tank. This unit is attached to a timer that is synchronized with a vent fan. The garden area is vented just before CO_2 is released.

▼ CO_2 generators harbor a propane or natural gas burner, pilot light, and control apparatus inside the vented, protective shroud.

◀ This atmospheric controller maintains a constant level of CO_2 in the garden room by controlling CO_2 production and venting the room.

CO_2 Emitter Systems

Use CO_2 emitter systems in small gardens where heat is a concern. Use an oscillating fan to mix CO_2 which is heavier than air.

CO_2 is metered out of a cylinder in a continuous flow or in bursts. Most suppliers exchange tanks and refill them. A steel tank containing 50 pounds of CO_2 weighs 170 pounds. An aluminum tank with 20 pounds of CO_2 weighs 50 pounds, and an aluminum tank full of 35 pounds of CO_2 weights 75 pounds.

CO_2 Generator Systems

Generators control CO_2 output with a pilot light, flow meter, and burner. They burn propane or natural gas and are best for large garden rooms. A burner creates CO_2 and water vapor as a by-product of burning oxygen from the air. One gallon of propane yields 36 cubic feet of gas and more than 100 cubic feet of CO_2. A cubic foot of propane gas yields three cubic feet of CO_2.

WHAT WILL YOU NEED?

Once you have made the decision to grow hydroponically, you must decide where you want to garden: indoors, in a greenhouse, or outdoors. Next you must decide how to control the garden atmosphere. The chart below will help you with the approximate cost of different items needed for each type of garden.

Check List	Cost	Indoor	Greenhouse	Outdoor	Buy
Hydroponic system	$30-$500	X	X	X	_____
pH meter	$30-100	X	X	X	_____
EC meter	$30-100	X	X	X	_____
Ventilation fan	$50-200	X	X		_____
Circulation fan	$20-100	X	X		_____
Thermometer	$5-30	X	X	X	_____
Hygrometer	$5-50	X	X	X	_____
Thermostat	$30-150	X	X		_____
Humidistat	$50-150	X	X		_____
Timer	$30-50	X	X		_____
Controller	$100-500	X	X		_____
CO_2	$200-400	X	X		_____
Air filter	$5-200	X	X		_____
				Total	_____

Bold indicates optional supplies.

CHAPTER THREE

Water, the 'universal solvent'; it provides a medium to transport nutrients required for plant life and makes them available for absorption by the roots. Water quality is essential to this process working at maximum potential.

Water & Nutrients

Plants absorb carbon, hydrogen, and oxygen from the air and the water. The rest of the elements, called nutrients, are absorbed from the nutrient solution, which is fertilizer diluted in water. The nutrient solution must have the proper balance of elements in order for the roots to be able to absorb nutrients efficiently.

Common tap water often contains high levels of sodium, calcium, alkaline salts, sulfur and chlorine. The pH could also be too high or too low. Water containing sulfur is easily smelled and tasted. Water in coastal areas often contains sodium. Regions with less than 20 inches of annual rainfall often suffer from water packed with alkaline salts.

Water quality is essential to a healthy hydroponic garden. Tap and well water, with less than 140 parts per million (PPM) of dissolved solids, is safe to grow plants hydroponically. Dissolved solids consist of minerals, such as calcium, magnesium, sodium, etc. Water with more than 50 PPM should be avoided because it causes countless problems.

Water containing more than 300 PPM dissolved solids must be filtered with a reverse-osmosis filter. Reverse osmosis forces 'tainted' water through a filter. A portion of the water comes out clean, and the dirty water is discarded.

▲ Look for signs of excess sodium and other dissolved solids in the water, such as the buildup of white salts on this shower head above.

▲ Check the EC and pH of water before mixing it with the fertilizer. If you do not have the proper meter, take your water to a hydroponic store to be tested.

◄ A reverse-osmosis filter system will turn tainted water into clean water.

pH

The pH is a scale from one to 14 that measures acid-to-alkaline balance. The pH reading of one is most acidic; seven, neutral; 14, most alkaline. Every full point change in pH signifies a 10-fold increase or decrease in acidity or alkalinity. Water with a pH of five is 10 times more acidic than water or soil with a pH of six. Water with a pH of five is 100 times more acidic than water with a pH of seven. Accurate pH measurement and control are essential to a strong, healthy garden.

If the pH is too low (acidic), acid salts bind nutrients chemically and the roots are unable to absorb them. High pH water and nutrient solutions cause nutrients to become unavailable. Toxic salt buildup also limits water uptake by roots. Most hydroponic plants grow well within a pH range of 5.5 to 6.5.

The pH in nutrient solutions can fluctuate a half point and not cause any problems, but larger deviations can affect element solubility. The pH of a buffered nutrient solution is more stable.

▲ This tester measures pH perpetually.

Roots take in nutrients at different rates which cause the ratios of nutrients in solution to change the pH. When the pH is above seven or below 5.5, some nutrients are not absorbed as fast as possible.

How pH Affects Nutrients

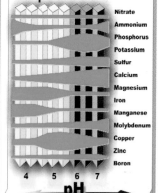

Nitrate
Ammonium
Phosphorus
Potassium
Sulfur
Calcium
Magnesium
Iron
Manganese
Molybdenum
Copper
Zinc
Boron

4   5   6   7
pH

Testing pH

Electronic pH testers are economical and convenient. Less expensive pH meters are accurate for casual use. More expensive models are quite accurate. The pH meters measure the electrical current between two probes. I prefer electronic pH meters over the reagent test kits and litmus paper. An electronic meter can measure pH thousands of times over while test kits are short lived.

▲ Test the pH of the nutrient solution.

Adjust nutrient solution pH levels with
pH Up or pH Down

Check the pH in the nutrient solution regularly.

pH Up

The pH in hydroponic systems often tends to drift down, because nutrients are naturally acidic. Add pH Up (usually potassium hydroxide) to the nutrient solution after mixing the nutrients to bring the pH back up to the desired level.

Measure the pH of the nutrient solution one hour after mixing, and change it to the desired level with pH Up or pH Down.

pH Down

Follow the directions on the container and mix pH adjuster into the reservoir slowly and completely.

Water that transports nutrient solution throughout plants transpires (evaporates) into the air, which can cause pH to climb and nutrient solution to become more concentrated. Add pH Down (usually, nitric or phosphoric acid) after mixing nutrients to bring the pH down to the desired level.

Buy pH up and pH down rather than making your own from concentrated acids. Commercial mixes are buffered and safe to use.

EC

EC,
PPM,
CF, TDS,
DS

Nutrient (fertilizer) concentrations are measured by their ability to conduct an electrical current. Pure water does not conduct electricity. Add nutrients (dissolved solids or salts) to the water and the solution will conduct electricity. The more fertilizer in the solution, the better it conducts electricity. The ability to conduct electrical current is called *Electrical Conductivity* (EC).

An EC reading will tell you the overall strength or concentration of dissolved solids in the solution. But an EC reading will not tell you the volume of each nutrient that is in the solution. EC is an overall measurement of the concentration of all the nutrients in the nutrient solution; for example, when you add fertilizer to pure water or a nutrient solution, the EC climbs.

Electrical conductivity is the most accurate scale to use to measure nutrient-solution strength. However, as the technology developed, several different scales were developed to measure EC, which include parts per million (PPM), conductivity factor (CF), total dissolved solids (TDS) and dissolved solids (DS). See Glossary of Terms. Each scale and manufacturer has its own idiosyncrasy.

▲ This meter measures EC perpetually.

▲ The Quick-Dip Thruegeon EC meter was one of the first easy-to-use durable testers.

▲ The Sal Testa measures EC and has a conversion chart on the back.

EC Meters

EC measurement is temperature sensitive. High-quality meters have automatic and manual temperature adjustments. Temperature must be factored into the EC reading to retain accuracy. For an accurate reading, make sure your nutrient solution and stock solution are at the same temperature. Inexpensive meters have a life span of about one year, and expensive meters can last for many years. The life of an EC meter, regardless of cost, is contingent upon regular maintenance. The probes must be kept moist and clean at all times. Watch for corrosion buildup on the probes of your meter. When probes are corroded, readings are not accurate.

How to take an EC measurement

To check the EC, collect a nutrient-solution sample from the reservoir. In growing mediums that hold nutrient solution – rockwool, coco coir, peat, etc. – collect a separate sample from within the medium. Collect samples with a syringe or turkey baster at least two inches deep in the growing medium. Place each sample in a clean jar. Use an EC meter to measure the samples. Under normal conditions, the EC in the growing medium should be a bit higher than the nutrient solution in the reservoir. If the EC of the solution drawn from the growing medium is substantially higher than the one from the reservoir, there is a nutrient (salt) buildup in the growing medium. Correct the imbalance by flushing the growing medium thoroughly with diluted nutrient solution, and replace it with fresh nutrient solution.

Save time and collect EC and pH samples simultaneously

As nutrients are added, electrical conductivity increases proportionally. Nutrient solutions generally range between 500 and 2000 parts per million (PPM). Most plants grow best within a PPM range of 800 to 1200.

Glossary of Terms

Electrical Conductivity (EC)

Conductivity Factor (CF)

Parts Per Million (PPM)

Total Dissolved Solids (TDS)

Dissolved Solids (DS)

Hydroponic Nutrients

Fertilizer

High quality hydroponic formulations are soluble and they contain all of the necessary nutrients and leave no impure residues. Manufacturers of high-quality fertilizers use food-grade nutrients in their formulations. There are many excellent commercial hydroponic fertilizers that contain nutrients in a balanced form to grow great hydroponic gardens. Hydroponic fertilizers are available in one- and two-part formulations that contain all of the nutrients necessary for rapid assimilation and growth. Low-quality fertilizers with impure components contain residue and sediments that build up and require extra maintenance. High quality soluble-hydroponic nutrients that are properly applied are immediately available for uptake by the roots.

▲ Today several manufacturers offer one-part hydroponic nutrient formulations. Many hydroponic gardeners prefer one-part solutions, because they require less mixing and are very easy to use.

◀ Two-part solutions separate macronutrients from micronutrients. These formulations offer more precise control of the nutrient solutions. See pages 30 to 33, for a complete explanation of macronutrients and micronutrients.

Call or go to a hydroponic store in your area and ask them for a fertilizer recommendation. These professionals will be able to steer you to the 'best mix' for your growing situation.

Technically, there is no difference between the chemicals that the plants use to manufacture food and grow; however, there is an ongoing debate as to the source of these chemicals and their ability to be absorbed by the plants. Organic advocates assure produce tastes better. See the following page for more information on organic nutrients.

Earth Juice organic nutrients

High Tide organic nutrient

Pure Blend organic nutrient

Hydro-Organic Fertilizers

Hydro-organic means 'growing plants without soil and feeding them with a soluble, organic liquid-nutrient solution.' Organic fertilizers are most often defined as 'containing substances with a carbon molecule or a natural unaltered substance, such as ground up rocks.'

Gardeners spend the time it takes to grow 'hydro' organically because natural nutrients bring out a delightful, organic taste in vegetables. To achieve a sweet, organic taste, nutrients must be soluble and readily available.

An exact balance of organic nutrients can be achieved with experimentation and attention to details. Even when using ready-mixed formulas, you may need to try different feeding schedules to get the exact dosage for best results.

Taking an accurate EC reading or mixing the exact amount of a specific nutrient is challenging in organic hydroponics. Chemical fertilizers are easy to measure and apply. Giving plants the specific amount of fertilizer they need for their stage of growth is easy.

Organic nutrients have a complex structure, and measuring the content is difficult. The pH and EC can also fluctuate. When shopping for organic nutrients, always buy from the same supplier and find out as much as possible about the source.

Mix soluble-organic fertilizers with other organic elements to make your own blend. Experiment and find the perfect mix for your system.

Additives

Additives, often called *bio-stimulants*, are products that make nutrients more readily available to plants, protect them from diseases and pests, or stimulate growth.

Liquid Humus

Bio-stimulants include the following: natural plant hormones, humic and fulvic acids, vitamins, microorganisms, proteins, and additional amino acids. Their combination and formulation dictates their results. Bio-stimulates can promote stronger roots, reduce stress and provide better use of nutrients, more efficient chlorophyll production, speed injury recuperation, and stronger germination.

Fulvic acid and humic acid are derived from soft coal (leonardite) and peat. Both are the result of plant composting. Fulvic acid is more plant reactive while humic acid acts more on growing mediums.

Kelp, the source of many plant hormones, is best when derived from cold-water extraction. Many hormones are destroyed if extracted from by-products of the food-processing industry.

Bio-Forte

Synergy

Bio-stimulants that contain microorganisms provide best results when applied frequently, because microorganisms existing in the growing medium will grow faster than the additives.

Proteins, amino acids, and vitamins also benefit the plants. However, the exact benefit of each is still being studied. Different mixes and concentrations give completely different results.

Always deal with a reputable supplier that can give you hands-on knowledge about the additive bio-stimulants they offer. Beware of outrageous claims that guarantee to solve every plant problem in the world.

The chart below is a guideline of satisfactory nutrient limits expressed in PPM. Do not deviate too far from these ranges to avert nutrient deficiencies and excesses.

ELEMENT	PPM Range	Average
Nitrogen	150-1000	250
Calcium	100-500	200
Magnesium	50-100	75
Phosphorus	50-100	80
Potassium	100-400	300
Sulfur	200-1000	400
Copper	0.1-0.5	0.05
Boron	0.5-5.0	1.0
Iron	2.0-10	5.0
Manganese	0.5-5.0	2.0
Molybdenum	0.01-0.05	0.02
Zinc	0.5-1.0	0.5

Nutrient Solution Composition

Soluble Salts Range Chart

Electrical conductivity (EC) as milli-siemen (mS) and total dissolved solids (TDS) as parts per million (PPM)

Range	Desirable	Permissible	Probable Salt Damage
		(but potential EC as mS concern)	
	0.75 to 2.0	2.0 to 3.0	3.0 and up

TDS as PPM			
	Desirable	Permissible	Probable Salt Damage
	500 to 1300	1300 to 2000	2000 and up

For nutrient solutions determinations one (1) mS (milli-siemen) or one mMho/cm^2 is equivalent to approximately 650 PPM total dissolved solids.

Nutrient Solutions

Change the nutrient solution every week, or at least every two weeks, to avoid toxic conditions and head-off nutrient excesses and deficiencies. Change the solution every week when plants are big. Plants absorb nutrients at different rates and some are used before others, which cause imbalances. The best form of preventative maintenance is to change the solution often. Skimping on fertilizer can cause stunted growth. Nutrient imbalances also cause the pH to fluctuate and usually drop.

Hydroponic System Maintenance

Check the hydroponic system regularly – pump, fittings, temperature, etc. – to ensure everything is working properly. High-performance systems require a high level of skill to achieve the best results. If a high-performance system malfunctions, plants can quickly feel the results; for example, if the electricity goes off, the pump breaks, the drain is clogged, or there is an imbalanced pH or EC, the consequences could be severe. A malfunction that lasts several days could stunt plants so badly that they take days or weeks to recover.

Change the nutrient solution every week for best results.

Nutrient Solution Maintenance

Plants use water rapidly, and the nutrient solution needs to be replenished regularly. Water is used at a much faster rate than nutrients. Casually, 'topping off' the reservoir with pH-balanced water will keep the solution relatively well balanced for a week or two. Never let the nutrient solution go for more than four weeks before draining the system and adding fresh, new solution. Smart gardeners change their solution every week. They flush the entire system with a mild nutrient-solution mix for a couple of hours between changing the reservoir.

Flushing with mild (quarter-strength or less) nutrient solution will actually remove more excess fertilizer than flushing the system with plain water.

Check the EC in the reservoir, growing medium, and runoff nutrient solution at the same time every day.

Use an electronic EC pen to monitor the level of dissolved solids in the solution. Occasionally, you will need to add some more fertilizer concentrate to maintain the EC level of the nutrient solution in the reservoir when 'topping off.' Keep the reservoir full at all times. The smaller the reservoir, the more rapid the depletion, and the more critical it is to keep full. Smaller reservoirs should be 'topped off' daily.

Mixing the Nutrient Solution

Make sure the reservoir is clean. When remixing the new nutrient solution, wipe or scrub out the excess salt buildup with a sponge, so that no residual salts or debris are present.

Starting with pure water will save time and energy when mixing and interpreting nutrient-solution effectiveness. If your input water contains more than 300 PPM of dissolved solids, use reverse osmosis to remove them.

Add the necessary amount of clean water to the reservoir. Determine the amount of nutrient necessary for the volume of water in the nutrient tank. Always follow the fertilizer's manufacturer's instructions. If you need help with the fertilizer dosage or use, contact the hydroponic professional where you bought the fertilizer. They have a complete knowledge of the products they offer the public.

Use accurate measuring containers when mixing nutrient solution.

Liquid fertilizers can be added directly to the water in the reservoir to form the nutrient solution. If using powders or crystal-hydroponic fertilizers, dissolve the crystals into a glass of warm (90-100°F) water and mix. Make sure the dry fertilizer is totally dissolved in water before adding to the pre-measured balance of water in the reservoir. This will ensure that the fertilizer and the water mix evenly. Stir the newly mixed fertilizer in the water to ensure they are totally blended together.

About an hour after mixing the nutrient solution, check the pH and EC. Add the appropriate amount of pH Up or pH Down to bring the pH to the desired level.

Check the pH and EC daily. Take regular pH and EC readings to help you keep the nutrient solution stable, so the garden can flourish.

Although this section may sound complex, it really is not. The background here will help you understand how and why nutrients act in plants. It will also provide you with much information when troubleshooting nutrient overdoses and deficiencies.

Nutrients and Macro Nutrients

Nutrients are elements that plants need to live. Carbon, hydrogen, and oxygen are absorbed from the air and the water. The rest of the elements, called nutrients, are absorbed from the growing nutrient solution.

Nutrients are supplied by the fertilizer dissolved in water, this forms the nutrient solution. There are at least 16 different nutrients that must be present in the nutrient solution for plants to flourish. These nutrients must be available in the proper balance in order for plant roots to be able to take them in.

Nutrients are grouped into two categories as follows: (1) Macronutrients include primary nutrients – nitrogen, phosphorus, and potassium – and secondary nutrients, which are calcium and magnesium; and (2) Micronutrients or trace elements, which are boron, chlorine, cobalt, copper, iron, manganese, molybdenum, selenium, silicon, sulfur and zinc. Each nutrient in the above categories can be further classified as either 'mobile' or 'immobile.'

Mobile nutrients re-translocate within a plant; they move to the specific part of the plant where they are needed and cause older leaves to show deficiencies first. Nitrogen, phosphorus, potassium, magnesium, and zinc are all mobile nutrients.

Immobile nutrients stay deposited in their original destination and cause new, young leaves to show deficiencies first. Calcium, boron, chlorine, cobalt, copper, iron, manganese, molybdenum, selenium, silicon, and sulfur are all immobile nutrients.

Nutrients

Macronutrients

Macronutrients are the elements that plants use most. Fertilizer is labeled to show micronutrients as nitrogen (N), potassium (P), and phosphorous (K) levels as 'N-P-K' percentages that appear as big numbers on the front of the package. They are always listed in the same N-P-K order. These nutrients must always be in an available form to supply the plants with the building blocks for rapid growth.

Nitrogen (N)

Plants love nitrogen and require high levels during vegetative growth and lower levels during the balance of life. Nitrogen washes away quickly and must be replaced regularly.

Hydroponic fertilizers commonly mix ammonium (NH_4+), which is readily available for uptake, but high concentrations can burn plants, and Nitrate (NO_3-) which is slower to assimilate.

Nitrogen-deficiency causes lower leaves to yellow between veins and later turn yellow all over. When severe, leaves die and drop off.

The early stage of nitrogen deficiency.

Phosphorus (P)

The highest levels of phosphorus are used during germination, seedling, cloning, and flowering stages. 'Super Bloom' fertilizers are designed for flowering and have high levels of phosphorus.

Lack of phosphorous will stunt plant growth. The leaves are smaller, bluish-green, and often with blotches. The older leaf tips turn dark. If severe, the leaf tips develop large, purplish-black dead blotches, then turn bronzish-purple, shrivel, and drop off.

The early stage of phosphorus deficiency.

Potassium (K)

Potassium is essential to the manufacture and movement of sugars and starches as well cell division. It increases chlorophyll, helps regulate stomata, disease resistance, encourages strong root growth and water intake.

Deficiency symptoms include tips and margins, followed by whole leaves that turn dark yellow and die. Stems often become weak and sometimes brittle.

The early stage of potassium deficiency.

Plants use large amounts of secondary nutrients. Fast-growing plants can process more secondary nutrients than some fertilizers can supply. High quality hydroponic fertilizers usually supply sufficient amounts.

Secondary Nutrients

Magnesium (Mg)

Plants use so much magnesium that deficiencies are common.

Deficiency causes lower leaves to develop yellow patches between veins. Rusty-brown spots appear on leaf margins, tips, and between veins as the deficiency progresses

The early stage of magnesium deficiency.

Calcium (Ca)

Most plants require nearly as much calcium as other macronutrients. Avert deficiencies by using soluble-hydroponic fertilizers containing adequate calcium.

Calcium deficiency is, somewhat, uncommon indoors. Leaves turn a very dark green and grow very slow. If severe, new growing shoots develop yellowish to purple hues and disfigure before shriveling up and dying.

The early stage of calcium deficiency.

Sulfur (S)

Many fertilizers contain some form of sulfur. Sulfur is seldom deficient. Avoid elemental (pure) sulfur in favor of sulfur compounds such as magnesium sulfate. Nutrients combined with sulfur mix better in water. Virtually, all ground, river, and lake water contains sulfate.

In cases of sulfur deficiency, young leaves turn a lime-green to yellowish color. Leaves yellow between veins and lack succulence. Veins remain green. It resembles a nitrogen deficiency.

The early stage of sulfur deficiency.

Micronutrients, also called trace elements, must be present in minute amounts and can reach toxic levels quickly. They function mainly as catalysts to plant processes and utilization of elements. Use high quality hydroponic fertilizers designed for hydroponic gardening to ensure a complete range of trace elements are available. Do not use an inexpensive fertilizer that does not list a specific analysis for each trace element on the label.

Micro-Nutrients

Zinc (Zn), iron (Fe), and manganese (Mn) are the three most common micronutrients found deficient. Deficiencies of any one of these three micronutrients cause problems in hydroponic gardens. Often, deficiencies of all three occur at the same time especially when growing medium or water pH is above 6.5.

Deficiencies of zinc, iron, and manganese are most common in arid climates – Southwestern USA, including California; Australia, and low-rainfall areas in Europe – where alkaline soil and alkaline water is common. All three have the same initial symptoms of deficiency: interveinal chlorosis of young leaves. It is often difficult to distinguish which element – zinc, iron, or manganese – is deficient; all three could be deficient. This is why treating the problem should include adding a chelated dose of all three nutrients.

Veins that remain green in between yellow margins could mean iron, manganese and zinc are deficient.

Summary

Water and fertilizers work hand-in-hand to provide many of the elements necessary for plant life. Water is often full of many dissolved solids. These dissolved solids are unknown mineral salts dissolved in the water.

If input water has more than 300 PPM dissolved solids and/or 50 PPM sodium, use a reverse-osmosis device to purify input water before adding fertilizers to make the nutrient solution. This simple act will help you avoid countless problems in the future by solving nutrient deficiencies before they occur. Strong, healthy plants also have few problems with pests and diseases.

Check the pH of input water before adding the fertilizer to form the nutrient solution. Fertilizers are naturally acidic and cause the pH of the nutrient solution to drop after combining with input water.

Correct the pH balance of the nutrient solution after adding fertilizer. Add pH Up or pH Down to bring the pH of the nutrient solution to 5.5 - 6.5, which is the 'safe' range for pH. Follow fertilizer's manufacturer's instructions on the label as to the exact level of pH.

Measure the EC or PPM of the nutrient solution regularly. Always check it at the same time of the day. Measure the EC of the input and runoff solution. There should be little difference between the two readings. If a large discrepancy exists, change the nutrient solution.

CHAPTER FOUR
GROWING MEDIUMS

A mass of roots cling to expanded clay on this harvested tomato plant.

Soilless growing mediums provide support for the root system; it holds and makes available oxygen, water, and nutrients. Three factors – texture, pH, and nutrient content – contribute to the roots' ability to grow in a substrate.

The texture of a substrate is governed by its size and structure. Proper texture promotes strong root penetration, oxygen retention, nutrient uptake and drainage. Large particles permit good aeration and drainage. Increased irrigation frequency is necessary to compensate for low water retention. Water, air-holding ability, and root penetration, are a function of texture. Smaller particles pack closer together and drain slower. Larger particles drain faster and retain more air.

Fibrous materials – vermiculite, peat moss, rockwool and coconut coir, etc. – retain much moisture within their cells. These substrates do not alter the composition of the nutrient solution. Such substrates are ideal for passive and ebb-and-flow hydroponic systems that absorb or 'wick up' nutrient solution via capillary action.

Washing or leaching built-up salts from fibrous growing mediums, after plants have been removed, can be laborious and time-consuming. These mediums – vermiculite, peat moss, rockwool and coconut coir – also loose some of their air-holding ability after a crop. Avoid such problems by replacing these substrates after use.

Mineral-growing mediums – expanded clay, perlite, pumice, gravel, sand, and pottery – are inert, meaning they do not react with living organisms or chemicals to change the integrity of the nutrient solution.

Wash built-up salts, root fragments, and other debris from mineral substrates to reuse. However, some mineral substrates, such as low quality expanded clay and fragile perlite, often shed so much dust that they deform and are unsuitable to reuse.

Rockwool

Rockwool is an inert, sterile, porous, non-degradable growing medium that provides firm root support. It is well suited for seedlings and cuttings, while larger slabs make attractive patio gardens.

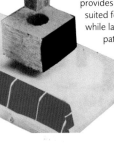

▲ Cubes come in a large variety of sizes.

Manufacturers offer bats or slabs, cubes, and bulk or granular flock. When saturated, rockwool contains about 80 percent nutrient solution, 15 percent air pore space, and five percent fiber.

Rockwool must be conditioned by soaking in a low-pH solution several hours, even overnight, to lower the naturally high pH.

▲ Rockwool seedling blocks fit into predrilled cubes and are transplanted onto slabs.

Quality rockwool is lightweight, and fibers can run both horizontally and vertically in slabs. The random orientation of the grain in rockwool flock promotes root growth in all directions. Flock can be either water absorbent or water-repellent.

A larger piece of rockwool makes a bigger reservoir to hold nutrient solution. Plants grown in rockwool do not suffer water stress until the rockwool is almost dry.

▲ Channels on the bottom of this rockwool block facilitate drainage.

▲ Rockwool slabs are wrapped in light-obscuring plastic to stop algae growth and create a container.

Coconut Fiber

Coconut fiber is also called palm peat, coco peat, cocos, kokos and coir. Coir is coconut pith, the fiber just under the green husk that has been soaked in water to remove salts, natural resins, and gums. Biodegradable coir holds much water while retaining its structure.

Quality washed pressed blocks and bricks are virtually inert with low-sodium content. Bricks weigh about 600 grams (1.3 pounds) to one kilogram (2.2 pounds). The pH is between 5.5 and 6.8.

▲ Compressed bricks of coco peat are convenient to transport and store. When wet, bricks expand to about eight times their original size.

▲ Coco peat is also available in slabs that are ready to grow, just add water.

Use coir alone or mix 50/50 with perlite or expanded clay to increase drainage. Sprinkle coconut coir on top of rockwool blocks to keep them from drying out.

Break dry bricks of coir apart by hand, or soak the bricks in water to expand to about 9 times original size. Get the most from coconut coir by keeping the grow-area air well circulated and ventilated.

▲ Loose coco peat is a good soil amendment or a stand-alone medium.

Expanded Clay

▲ Cuttings will be ready to transplant when roots dangle from expanded clay pellets.

Expanded clay pellets are lightweight, inert, pH neutral, and reusable. Air pores, inside the round pellets, with a sturdy outer ceramic shell, create a growing medium with excellent nutrient solution holding ability. The round shape allows plenty of air to reside between pellets to stimulate nutrient uptake as well as allow ample drainage.

Mix with other mediums, such as peat and coco coir, to increase drainage as well as disperse nutrient solution. Place on top of growing mediums to retain moisture and keep algae from growing.

Expanded clay is popular in Hydroculture hydroponic systems used in many office buildings, hotels, and public buildings. It is especially well suited for plants that require good drainage, such as roses.

Sold in various diameters and brand names, such as LECA, Geolite, Hydroton, etc. Expanded clay is also referred to as expanded clay pebbles, expanded aggregate, or expanded rock.

▲ To reuse, toss expanded clay on a screen and wash away debris with plenty of fresh water.

▲ The porous interior makes expanded clay light and able to hold air and nutrient solution.

◀ Adult peppers in expanded clay are setting buds and peppers already!

Soilless Mix

‣ Perlite is sand or volcanic glass expanded by heat, like popcorn. It holds water and nutrients on its many irregular surfaces. Versatile perlite is available in three main grades: fine, medium and coarse. Mix up to one-third with absorbent substrates to improve drainage and aeration.

‣ Vermiculite is mica processed and expanded by heat. It holds water, nutrients, and air within its fibers and gives body to fast-draining soils. Used in hydroponic wick systems; vermiculite holds and wicks much moisture. Available in three grades: fine, medium, and coarse. Use 'fine' as an ingredient in cloning mixes and 'coarse' as a soil amendment.

‣ Peat moss is partially decomposed vegetation mined from vast, cold, and wet bogs. Sphagnum and hypnum peat are used to amend soil and as a growing medium. It is difficult to wet the first time. Mix peat moss with other components before wetting. The pH ranges from 3-5 and could drop after decomposing. Once wet, the inert peat moss retains 15 to 30 times its weight in moisture.

Pottery

Pumice

Synthetic Foam

Nut Husk Peat

Peat Perlite Mix

More Growing Mediums

◀ **Pottery** can be a hydroponic medium, although heavy, it is inert, holds air, drains well, and is often free. It holds moisture, nutrient, and oxygen on its outer surfaces.

◀ **Pumice** or volcanic rock is porous and lightweight. It holds moisture and air in the catacomb-like surfaces. It occasionally floats and sharp edges can grind on roots if moved.

◀ **Synthetic foam** can also be a hydroponic growing medium. Bats hold air, moisture, and nutrients within the cells. Manufacturers tout this substrate because it can be reused.

◀ **Peat** mixed with nut husks and other derivatives is economical. This mix takes advantage of the husk by-product, which adds extra drainage and air-holding ability to the substrate.

◀ **Perlite** is often mixed with coconut coir or peat moss to increase drainage and aeration. It can be mixed in various percentages to achieve a different effect that benefits specific plants.

CHAPTER FIVE

Different Systems

▶ The growing medium provides air and wicks up the nutrient solution in the Luwasa hydroculture system.

Wick

Hydroponic systems are distinguished by the way the nutrient solution is applied. Systems are either 'passive' or 'active'. Passive gardens, such as wick and Luwasa hydroculture systems, rely on capillary action to transfer the nutrient solution from the reservoir to the growing medium. Active hydroponic systems actively move nutrient solution into contact with the growing medium and roots. Once the nutrient solution is delivered, it is recovered and reused or discarded.

In a Luwasa hydroculture system, nutrient is absorbed by the roots and is wicked up to the growing medium: expanded clay pellets. In a wick system, the nutrient solution is absorbed by a wick and transported to the growing medium and roots via capillary action. Absorbent-growing mediums – vermiculite, peat moss, coir, and rockwool – are ideal for passive wick systems. Wick and Luwasa systems are ideal for slow growing and low maintenance perennial plants, such as philodendrons, Benjamin figs, African violets, etc. Wick systems are inexpensive to set up, require no pump, and have no moving parts. It is important to choose the proper growing medium for the plants you are growing because it can stay very wet, causing less air to be available to speed nutrient uptake.

◀ Air Table garden by Terraponics is operated with a solar-powered 12-volt pump and was left unattended for 30 days.

Air Table

Air Tables are simple, easy-to-use hydroponic gardens that are appealing to novice and experienced gardeners alike. The unique operating principle is simple, efficient and nearly fail proof. The nutrient solution is forced up to the growing bed with air pressure generated by an external air pump. Once flooded, the nutrient solution stays in the growing bed for a few minutes before it drains back into the reservoir. Constant air pressure during flooding also aerates the growing medium. The sealed, airtight reservoir limits evaporation, which prevents algae growth and keeps the nutrient fresh. The external pump reduces the overall price of the system and helps prevent electrical shock and mishaps. You can use rockwool, coco coir, peat, or a composite growing medium with excellent results.

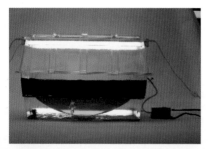

◀ The clear reservoir shows how air pressure moves the blue-colored nutrient solution up into the black growing bed. This 28 x 9 x 10-inch garden automatically waters plants with precision and a minimum of guesswork. The hydroponic system is ideal for gardeners with a busy lifestyle.

Water Culture

Water culture says it all. Water is the actual growing medium. Plants are held in net pots full of expanded clay pellets. Net pots are nestled in the 'access lid' that covers the reservoir/growing bed. Small seedlings or cuttings with short roots dangle in the nutrient solution. A submersible pump aerates the nutrient solution. The net pots are actually submerged in the aerated nutrient solution. A four-inch hole in the center of the access lid makes checking the pump, roots, and solution quick and easy. Roots easily absorb the exact amount of nutrient solution in the oxygenated environment.

Simple-by-design, no timers are required because the pump is on 24 hours a day. This low-maintenance garden is perfect for casual gardeners as well as the hydroponic enthusiast. The operating principle is simple, effective, and grows plants non-stop.

1   Small plants are grown in net pots and set into the access lid or growing bed.

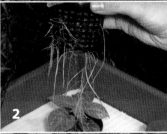

2   Small pepper plants develop quickly in this system.

3   Within a short time, there is a mass of roots on this plant that will soon produce a heavy crop of garden-fresh basil.

4   The massive roots on these pepper plants take in the exact amount of nutrients needed to produce a bountiful harvest.

◄ The nutrient solution is pumped into the table and drains back into the reservoir. An overflow keeps the solution in check.

Ebb-and-Flow Systems

Ebb and flow, also known as flood and drain, hydroponic systems are low maintenance and easy to use. Individual plants, in pots or grow cubes, are set on a table or growing bed that can hold an inch or two of water. Nutrient solution is periodically pumped into the growing bed. The bed is flooded from the bottom. Oxygen-poor air is forced out by the nutrient solution as it wets the growing medium. Once the nutrient solution reaches a set level, an overflow pipe drains the excess to the reservoir. When the pump is turned off, the growing medium drains. This draws in new, oxygen-rich air into contact with the roots. A maze of channels directs the runoff solution back into the catchment tank or reservoir. This cycle is repeated several times a day. Ebb-and-flow systems are ideal for growing many short plants.

◄ The ebb-and-flow tables allow excess water to flow away from the growing medium and roots.

▶ Rockwool blocks or containers filled with growing medium are set on the growing table, and small plants in root cubes are set into the holes in the blocks. Transplanting is simple, clean, and painless.

1   Small seedlings and cuttings are grown in small grow cubes. When the plant and roots are developed, they are set in the tray above. Roots dangle and grow in the tray that is flooded below.

2   The drain plug, on the front of the reservoir below this crop of basil, makes changing the nutrient solution quick and easy.

3   Growing a perpetual crop of seedlings, small plants, or cuttings is easy in an ebb-and-flow garden.

4   Nutrient solution is pumped up into the bed via the short fixture on the left. The overflow fitting on the right guarantees the nutrient solution will not spill over the top of the growing bed. When the irrigation cycle is complete, the solution drains back through the short fixture.

5   Self-leveling legs, similar to those of a washing machine, ensure all plants receive an even dose of nutrient solution and that it all drains back into the reservoir below.

Top-Feed Bucket Systems

Nutrient solution in a top-feed bucket system is delivered to the base of individual plants via spaghetti tubing or an emitter that meters out a specific dose. The aerated nutrient solution flows over the growing medium and roots. The nutrient solution is directed back to the reservoir when it drains from the growing medium. Rockwool, coco coir, expanded clay, and composite soilless mixes are the most common growing mediums found in top-feed systems.

Top-feed bucket systems can be used with individual containers, long beds, or tables. Large plants grow best in systems with several gallons of growing medium to support roots. Small containers are perfect for smaller plants.

Buckets can be connected together with a feeding manifold and drainage system. Individual containers are easily moved to fit the allotted space. Plants can also be transplanted or removed from pots and cared for individually.

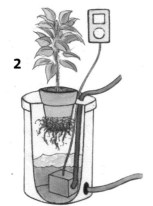

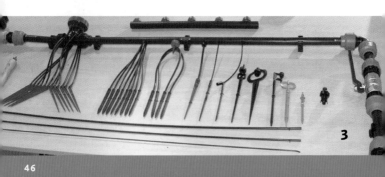

1 Various emitters are available to apply nutrient solution. A single application point works well in absorbent rockwool and coco coir. Expanded clay works best when the nutrient solution is applied via a large round emitter, several single emitters, or a spray emitter.

2 This cutaway of a top-feed bucket system shows how roots dangle in a 100 percent humid environment before growing into the nutrient solution.

3 An array of emitters connected to a main manifold shows the different types available. Across the bottom are three diameters of spaghetti tubes that dispense different volumes of nutrient solution.

4 The reservoir is directly under the growing containers. Square containers maximize root space. The emitters spray streams of nutrient solution to ensure even penetration of the growing medium.

5 Self-contained, top-feed buckets consist of a growing container nestled inside a reservoir containing a pump. Easy-to-move systems are perfect to grow large, single plants.

6 Roots grow down into the nutrient solution to form a mass on the bottom. Irrigation from the top circulates aerated nutrient solution and flushes out old oxygen-poor solution.

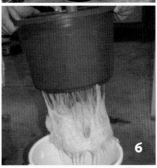

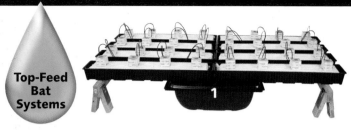

Top-Feed Bat Systems

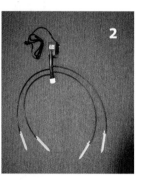

Top-feed bat (slab) systems are productive and easy to maintain. Top-feed bat systems are popular with home gardeners and commercial greenhouse growers alike. The nutrient solution is delivered via spaghetti tubes from the top. An emitter is attached to the spaghetti tube so that a specific dose of nutrient solution is metered to each plant. The nutrient solution is aerated, as it is applied and absorbed by the growing medium, before flowing downward to the reservoir.

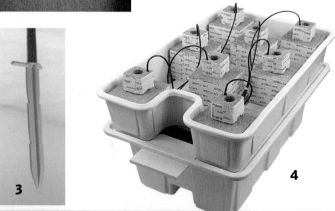

1 Rockwool bats are placed in individual drainage trays. The nutrient solution is pumped from the reservoir below and delivered to the plants above via spaghetti tubes that are attached to emitters that are fixed in the rockwool cubes.

2 A simple nutrient-solution delivery manifold is connected to the spaghetti tubes that are attached to the emitters. The tubes are attached to a short manifold that is fed by a pump submerged in a reservoir.

3 Emitters are designed to be anchored in the growing medium and emit a specific dose of nutrient solution.

4 Individual blocks in this rockwool system allow gardeners the ability to remove or change plants, if necessary.

5 Nutrient solution is pumped via spaghetti tubes from the reservoir below and distributed via the emitters pressed into rockwool cubes.

6 A nice crop of peppers is growing in this recently planted top-feed bat system.

7 This cutaway drawing shows how nutrient delivery is simple and easy with a top-feed bat system. Aerated nutrient solution is metered via an emitter onto a grow cube. Aerated solution percolates down through the medium. Channels in the bottom of the tray speed drainage back into the reservoir.

5

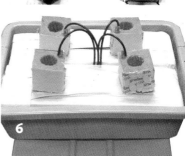

6

7

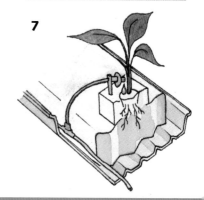

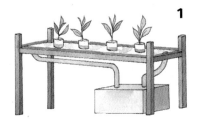

1

NFT Systems

High-performance Nutrient Film Technique (NFT) systems are for expert gardeners. Once a seedling or cutting has developed a strong root system, they are placed in the growing channel or gully. Tender roots hang down onto capillary matting that is placed on the bottom of a gully. Constantly, aerated nutrient solution flows rapidly from one end of the gully, down around, and over the roots to the other end.

Irrigation is often constant, 24 hours a day. Roots absorb virtually all the oxygen and nutrients they need. When fine-tuned, growth is extremely fast. However, NFT systems offer little buffering ability. In the absence of a growing medium, roots must be bathed in aerated solution constantly. A failed pump or clogged system causes problems fast.

2

3

1 Nutrient solution travels a circular path in an NFT system. Pumped from the reservoir to the gullies, the solution flows over the roots and back to the reservoir. Proper gully incline, volume, and the flow of the nutrient solution are key elements in NFT gardens.

2 Small net pots are preferred for most NFT systems. Larger net pots are used in NFT systems as well as top-feed hydroponic systems.

3 Rockwool blocks or net containers are set on shallow gullies irrigated with multiple streams, via a manifold, to assure even nutrient-solution penetration.

4 The nutrient solution is pumped from the reservoir into inclined gullies via a manifold and tubing at the upper end. Aerated nutrient solution flows quickly over the roots. A drain directs the nutrient back into the reservoir.

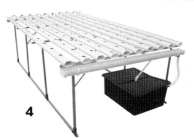

4

Gully 1 ▸
The ribs below the gully provide support on long runs and the central channels direct the nutrient solution.

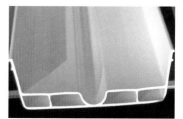

Gully 2 ▸
Ribbed gully directs the nutrient solution evenly, and channels on the sides guide the excess solution and provide support.

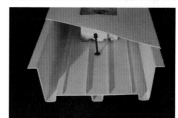

Gully 3 ▾
The stand-alone gully, with a concave bottom, allows nutrient solution flow.

A popular variation of an NFT system is the top-feed gully system. The nutrient solution is applied from the top of each plant container via an irrigation manifold. More irrigation sites help each plant receive proper irrigation.

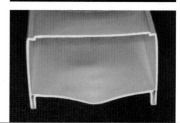

▲ This aeroponic garden facilitates exceptionally fast root development and plant growth.

Aeroponics

Aeroponic systems use no growing medium and offer the highest performance possible. Roots are suspended in a dark growth chamber without growing medium, where they are misted with oxygen-rich nutrient solution at regular intervals. The humidity in the chamber remains near 100 percent. Roots have the maximum potential to absorb nutrients in the presence of air. Only air and nutrient solution fill the growth chamber. Plants are often grown in net pots full of growing medium. Virtually unlimited access to oxygen gives roots the maximum potential to absorb nutrients and grow at a phenomenal rate.

Aeroponic systems require greater attention to detail. No growing medium acts as a water/nutrient bank, and the system can be delicate to use. If the pump fails, roots soon dry and the plants suffer. Systems that use delicate spray nozzles must be kept free of debris. Imbalanced nutrient solution and pH can also cause problems in short order. This is why it is important to purchase quality components or a ready-made system from a qualified source.

Some manufacturers offer hybrid aeroponic/NFT systems. These systems support a series of misting nozzles inside of a growing bed or gully. Roots are misted with nutrient solution that is pumped from a reservoir. The solution drains away via the bed or gully and back into a reservoir.

◄ Long root systems develop quickly on cuttings in this aeroponic system.

Aquaponics

Aquaponics is a combination of hydroponics and aquaculture: fish farming. In this symbiotic relationship, fish waste provides a food source for growing the plants; and the plants supply a natural filter for fish. This managed ecosystem is becoming increasingly popular as food sources and groundwater have become increasingly tainted. Aquaponics is an ideal answer to recycle nutrient-rich 'fishy' water and the hydroponic enthusiasts' need for nutrient-rich solution. The best part in this environmental and friendly system is that everything is organic with no chemicals added!

Still in its infancy, aquaponics is following a steady upward growth curve. The obvious hydroponic benefits: elimination of fertilizer costs and associated labor. The dramatic reduction of the filtration of fish waste is the main benefit afforded in aquaculture.

A home aquarium, with either ornamental fish or food fish, is easy to merge with a small hydroponic system to grow garden-fresh herbs, vegetables, and flowers. Backyard gardeners are already setting up aquaponic systems that supply enough fish and produce for their family.

For more information on aquaponics, see the *Aquaponics Journal* available at www.aquaponics.com.

▲ A compact-fluorescent lamp illuminates a crop of lettuce floating in a small ornamental fish aquarium. Lettuce is nourished exclusively by fish waste.

▲ A 500-gallon tank full of fish supplies nutrients via fish waste to fancy lettuce growing in an NFT-aquaponic system.

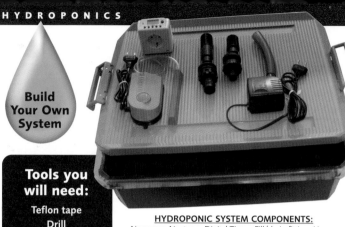

Build Your Own System

Tools you will need:

Teflon tape
Drill
Large hole-drill bits
Pocketknife
Sharpie
Marker

HYDROPONIC SYSTEM COMPONENTS:

Air pump; Air stone; Digital Timer; Fill/drain fitting; Heavy-duty flat or tub (garden bed); Heavy-duty lid to fit reservoir; Heavy-duty tub (reservoir) ; Overflow fitting; Reservoir; Reservoir lid; Submersible pump 70 GPH; Supply tubing

This garden is very simple and easy to build. Most well-equipped discount building centers have all the parts, except for the fill/drain and the overflow fittings.

I used a large nursery flat with a solid bottom and a plastic container from a discount store. The reservoir container was clear, so I had to paint the outside black. The nutrient solution must be kept in the dark to prevent algae growth.

To build, drill two holes near the center of the garden bed big enough to accommodate the fill/drain and the overflow fittings. Once drilled, set the garden bed on the reservoir lid. Use a Sharpie or indelible ink to mark the position of the holes. Drill larger holes in the top of the reservoir lid.

▾ Different size containers fit in the ebb-and-flow table.

Insert the intake and the overflow fittings. Wrap threads with Teflon tape before securing them in place.

Connect the hose to the pump and the fill/drain fitting. Connect the air stone to the air pump and place stone in reservoir with air stone pump outside.

The reservoir should hold 2-3 times as much nutrient solution as it takes to flood the garden bed. To start, set the digital timer to water four times a day for 10-minute cycles. Never let watering time exceed 30 minutes, from the time the pump starts until all the solution has drained into the reservoir.

The system can be filled with containers full of expanded clay, coco coir, rockwool flock, rockwool blocks, etc.

▾ Nursery flat, before drilling two holes near the center.

▸ Use a hole-drill bit to cut a hole in the bottom of the nursery flat.

◂ Once holes are drilled, set nursery flat over the top of the reservoir. Mark a bull's-eye in the middle of each hole. These marks will serve as the center of the holes in the reservoir lid.

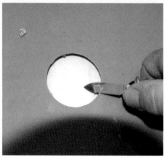

◀ Make the holes in the reservoir lid big enough for the bottom of the fill/drain and overflow fittings to fit through.

▶ Overflow fitting on the left and fill/drain fitting on the right.

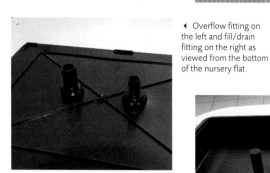

◀ Overflow fitting on the left and fill/drain fitting on the right as viewed from the bottom of the nursery flat.

▶ Overflow fitting on the left and fill/drain fitting on the right.

▸ View from the bottom of the reservoir lid of fill/drain fitting on the left and overflow fitting on the right.

◂ View from under reservoir lid of overflow fitting on left and on the right, a pump attached to fill/drain fitting with green supply tubing.

▸ Ebb-and-flow reservoir on bottom covered with a blue reservoir lid. A nursery flat is used as a fill-and-drain table. Near the center of the table, an overflow fitting on the left and a fill/drain fitting on the right can be seen. Different sized containers fill the growing table.

Reservoirs

◀ Keeping reservoirs covered will diminish evaporation, algae growth, and other problems.

◀ A simple float valve will keep reservoirs replenished with water automatically.

▶ Keep nutrient solution at 55° to 60° F for best results.

75   24
70   21
65   18
60   16
55   13
50   10
F°   **C°**

The reservoir contains the nutrient solution and should be as big as possible. Plants use much more water than nutrients. Water transpires via leaves and evaporates into the air.

Fast-growing plants can use a quart or more of water daily. As water is used, the concentration of fertilizer in the solution increases, there is less water and nearly the same amount of nutrients. Water must be replenished to account for this imbalance.

A float valve will control the level of water in the reservoir. A 'full' line on the inside of the reservoir shows when the solution is low. Add water when the solution level drops, daily if necessary.

Reservoir temperature

Keep the nutrient-solution temperature between 55° and 60°F for best results. If temperature is a problem, ask your hydroponic professional for reservoir heaters and coolers.

A 55° to 60°F (13° to 16°C) solution helps control transpiration and humidity, as well as assist nutrient uptake. A submerged air stone moderates temperature differential between the ambient air and the reservoir and increases oxygen content. Solution temperatures in excess of 75°F promote rot and disease.

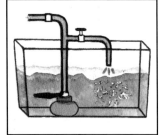

▲ This ingenious setup provides extra aeration to the reservoir.

Pumps

Pumps are necessary for active hydroponic systems that move nutrient solution into contact with plant roots. Pumps are rated in the amount of liquid they move over time, such as gallons per hour (GPH) or liters per hour (LPH).

Non-submersible pumps are less expensive, but they cannot be immersed inside the nutrient solution of the nutrient reservoir. Such pumps should also be well sealed to avoid electrical shock or malfunction in humid or wet garden-room environments.

Submersible pumps are sealed, and the internal components are usually bathed in long-lasting oil. The oil lubricates the moving parts and cools the pump. Versatile submersible pumps can be placed inside the nutrient solution of the reservoir or mounted outside the reservoir. Always look for high-quality pumps recommended by your hydroponic retailer that are guaranteed. Submersible pumps should not corrode or 'bleed off' any elements harmful to the plants.

The pump should be set up to lift the solution out of the reservoir. Set the reservoirs up high enough so 'spent' nutrient solution can siphon or gravity-flow into a drain or the outdoor garden.

▲ This small pump is sufficient for many different, small hydroponic gardens. The foam filter helps keep the delivery system from clogging.

▶ Larger pumps cost a little more and add pressure and volume to nutrient-delivery systems.

Which System is Best for You?

Which hydroponic system is right for you? Consider the features and choose a system that fits your lifestyle and budget. All prices and times are approximate and will vary according to manufacturer and skill level. Hydroponic enthusiasts often spend much time with their gardens because they are so interesting and fun!

Hydro. System	Wick or Luwasa	Air Table	Water Culture
Cost	$5-$50	$400	$50-$100
Skill level	Low	Low	Low
Setup	5-30 minutes	15 minutes	15 minutes
Maintenance	15 min./week	15-30 min./week	15 min./week
Space	Small	Small	Small
Application	Slow-Growing Plants	Fast-Growing Plants	Fast/Slow-Growing Plants

Hydro. System	Flood/drain	Top-Feed Bucket	Top-Feed Bats
Cost	$50-500	$50-500	$50-$500
Skill level	Medium	Medium	Medium
Setup	15-120 minutes	15-120 minutes	15-120 minutes
Maintenance	15-60 min./week	15-60 min./week	15-60 min./week
Space	Small/Large	Small/Large	Small/Large
Application	Fast-Growing Plants	Fast-Growing Plants	Fast-Growing Plants

Hydro. System	NFT	Aeroponics	Aquaponics
Cost	$300+	$300+	$400+
Skill level	High	High	High
Setup	30-120 min./week	30-120 min./week	60-120 min./week
Maintenance	15 min./week	15 min./week	15 min./week
Space	Medium/Large	Small/Large	Small/Large
Application	Fast-Growing Plants	Fast-Growing Plants	Fast-Growing Plants

Note: All prices and times are estimated.

SEEDS TO FLOWERS

A seed contains all of the genetic characteristics of a plant and dictates a plant's size, disease and pest resistance; root, stem, leaf, flower and fruit production, and many other traits.

A seed contains an embryo, including the genes, and a supply of food wrapped in a protective outer coating. Soft pale or green seeds are usually immature and should be avoided. Fresh, dry, and mature seeds less than a year old, sprout quickly and grow robust plants. Store seeds in a cool, dark, and dry place. Some seeds will remain viable for five years or longer.

Once a strong root system is established and foliage growth increases rapidly, seedlings enter the vegetative-growth stage. A vegetative plant will produce as much foliage as light, CO_2, nutrients, and water will permit. High levels of nitrogen are needed – potassium, phosphorus, calcium, magnesium, sulfur, and trace elements – are used at a faster rate, too.

▲ Seeds carry the genetic code to make a plant.

Long-day plants require 16 to 18 hours of light per day: such plants – tomatoes, peppers, pansies, African violets, etc. – will continue vegetative growth as well as flower and fruit formation under this light regimen.

Short-day plants – poinsettias, Christmas cactus, Napa cabbage, chrysanthemums, etc. – will stay in the vegetative stage under 18 hours of light. Some gardeners even keep the light on 24 hours a day! Flowering is induced in short-day plants under 12 hours of light and 12 hours of darkness every 24 hours.

▲ This basil plant is in the green, leafy vegetative-growth stage.

◀ This fruiting pepper plant flourishes in a hydroponic soilless mix.

▲ Soak seeds in water 12 to 24 hours before planting in growing medium.

▲ Or set seeds on a moist paper towel and keep them evenly moist. A white taproot will appear in a few days.

Starting Seedlings

Seeds need water, heat, and air to germinate. Most seeds sprout without light in two to seven days in temperatures from 70°-90° F. Germination is fastest when the growing medium is between 75°-80° F and the air temperature is at 70° F.

Water seedlings every one to three days, and keep evenly moist. Let excess water drain away freely. The seed contains an adequate 'food supply' for germination. Watering with a mild-fertilizer mix will hasten growth. Prevent fungus by watering with a mild, two-percent bleach or fungicide solution.

▲ Plant the soaked or sprouted seed in moist rockwool blocks. If planting delicate-sprouted seed, handle with care and point taproot downward.

When the plant sprouts upward and out of the grow cube, place it under a fluorescent lamp or low-light source.

Transplant peat pellets and root cubes in two to three weeks, when the roots show through the sides. Upon transplanting, feed with a diluted fertilizer solution.

Over-watering is the biggest obstacle most growers face when growing seedlings. Keep the growing medium uniformly moist and not waterlogged.

▸ Or sow soaked or sprouted seed directly in moist peat pellet or other growing medium without soaking.

▾ Once planted slightly under the surface, cover and press lightly. Water again and drain excess water from tray. Keep the planting medium evenly moist.

▸ Plant fragile 'root tip' of sprouted cucumber seed facing down.

▾ Seedling cucumber shows oval-shaped cotyledon leaves (upper leaves) and the first 'true leaf' below them.

▴ Cucumber seedling emerges from peat pellet.

Starting Cuttings

Plants can be reproduced (propagated) sexually or asexually. Seeds are the product of sexual propagation, and cuttings are the result of asexual or vegetative propagation. Taking a cutting, sometimes called a clone, is cutting a growing branch tip and rooting it.

A cutting is an exact-genetic replica of the 'mother' or 'parent plant.' Any plant can become a mother to supply cutting stock, whether grown from seed or a cutting. Always start with the best parent plants you can find.
The genetic characteristics, growth habits of strong or weak parents, are passed on to cuttings.

▲ This small 'mother plant' will soon turn into a tray of cuttings.

▲ Giving cuttings a small amount of a supplement, such as SuperThrive, or a product that contains vitamin B1 will help overcome the shock of being cut.

Getting Ready

Any plant can become a cutting regardless of age or growth stage. For best results, take cuttings from plants at least two months old.

Cuttings develop a dense root system quickly when stems have a high carbohydrate and low-nitrogen concentration. Build carbohydrate levels by leaching the growing medium with an abundance of water to flush out the nutrients. Older leaves may turn a light green color. Carbohydrate content is highest in lower, older, more mature branches.

While rooting, cuttings require minimum nitrogen and increased phosphorus to initiate and promote root growth. Make sure 'parent plants' are strong and healthy before cutting and avoid spraying them with pesticides or fungicides.

Making cuttings is the most shocking event any plant can suffer. To survive, the stem that grew leaves must now grow roots. Speed this process with rooting hormones.

▲ Clonex is the original rooting hormone gel. Gardeners prefer cloning gels, because the rooting hormones spread evenly and the gel stays on the stem.

Rooting Hormones

Root-inducing hormones are available in powders; however, liquid and gel types are the most versatile and they penetrate stems evenly and are consistent.

Do not dip cuttings into the original hormone container. Pour a small amount into a separate container and throw away any excess so as not to contaminate the original solution.

Warning: Use only root hormones approved for edible plants.

▲ Olivia's Cloning Solution is a very popular liquid-rooting hormone.

Taking Cuttings Step-by-Step

1. Prepare to take cuttings. Set out a knife, cutting gel and container, chop stick, grow cubes, cutting dome, and tray.

2. Select a nice growing tip to cut.

3. Use a sharp blade to make a 45-degree cut below the leaf/branch internodes. The cutting should be 2 to 4 inches long.

4. Trim the bottom leaves from the cut branch.

5. Make clean cuts with the sharp knife.

6. Make a hole, a little larger than the stem, in the rooting cube with a chopstick or something similar.

7. Dip trimmed cutting in the liquid-rooting hormone or gel.

8. Insert the hormone-coated stem into the pre-made hole.

9. Water the cuttings with very mild nutrient solution.

10. Place cuttings under humidity dome to retain moisture.

Most cuttings root fastest with the following steps:

• Eighteen - 24 hours of fluorescent light.

• The growing medium is kept at 80° F and the ambient-air temperature stays 5° F cooler.

• Humidity levels are 95 to 100 percent the first two days and gradually reduced to 85 percent over seven days.

A few more hints:

• Mist cuttings with water. This also cools foliage and slows transpiration to help traumatized cuttings retain moisture.

• Some cuttings may wilt but regain rigidity in a few days.

• Do not tug on cuttings to see if they are rooted.

• Roots should be visible through rooting cubes in one to three weeks.

Vegetative Growth

Once a strong root system is established and foliage growth increases rapidly, seedlings enter the vegetative-growth stage. When chlorophyll production is full-speed ahead, a vegetative plant will produce as much green, leafy foliage as light, CO_2, nutrients, and water permit. A strong, unrestricted root system is essential to supply much needed water and nutrients. Unrestricted vegetative growth is the key to large, radiant flowers and strong, flavorful fruit. Nutrient and water needs and intake change during vegetative growth. Transpiration is carried on at a more rapid rate than during seedling growth, which requires more water. High levels of nitrogen are needed – potassium, phosphorus, calcium, magnesium, sulfur and trace elements – are used at much faster rates. The larger a plant gets, the bigger the root system, the more nutrient solution and water it will use.

1 These good-looking pepper plants still produce vegetative growth when the first flowers start to appear.

2 Plants in this beautiful indoor hydroponic garden are in full vegetative growth.

3 Young vegetative pepper plants in a rockwool slab system.

4 This lettuce was harvested when still in the vegetative-growth stage.

Flowering and Fruiting

Vibrant flowers, delicious vegetables, and fresh fruits are some of the rewards for growing a hydroponic garden. During flowering, plants require less nitrogen and more phosphorus and potassium and some plants require more calcium, too. Use a 'bloom' formula for best results. As plants produce more flowers and fruit, they use more nutrient solution. Gardeners often harvest the best tomatoes, peppers, eggplants, etc., by increasing the nutrient-solution strength incrementally until harvest. Check with your hydroponic professional for specific recommendations.

Taste-conscious hydroponic gardeners often rinse the nutrient solution from the plants by flushing the system with plain water seven to ten days before harvest. To get more growth, drain the reservoir, and run a 'final flush' or a 'clearing solution' in the system. Such products flush nutrients out from the plants much more quickly.

1   Clearing Solution washes away hydroponic nutrients from plants before harvest.

2   Large, thick-walled peppers grow where flowers sprouted. These peppers will continue to flower and fruit for many months.

3   Short-day snapdragons flower under 12 hours of light and 12 hours of darkness.

4   Tomato plants will produce vine-ripened fruit for months in hydroponics.

Garden Schedule and Checklist

Weekly Checklist
Check the following to see if they function properly:

	Daily	Weekly
Air Ventilation - Regular, New, Fresh Air	X	
Air Circulation - Leaves Flutter in Wind	X	
Humidity – 40 to 50 Percent	X	
Temperature: Day, 70° to 75° F., Night, 55° to 60° F	X	
Irrigation Schedule	X	
Check Irrigation Fittings		X
Check pH	X	
Check EC	X	
Change Nutrient Solution		X
Check for Spider Mites and Insects		X
Check for Disease and Fungus		X
Check for Nutrient Deficiencies		X
Check Walls and Ceiling for Mold		X
Move Lamp Up, 12 to 36 Inches Above Plants		X
Check Electrical Connections for Heat		X
Cleanup!	X	X

Prevention

Cleanliness is the key to insect and fungus prevention. Keep floor, ground, and substrate surfaces clean. Gardeners and their tools often transport many microscopic pests and diseases. These are easily avoided with simple cleanliness.

Wearing clean clothes and using clean tools will help reduce problems. A separate set of indoor tools is easy to keep clean. Pests and diseases ride from plant to plant on dirty tools.

Wash your hands after handling diseased plants. Do not walk around the buggy outdoor garden and then visit the indoor garden. Even walking across a lawn or brushing up against outdoor plants could transport pests and diseases to your indoor garden. Contact with dogs, cats, and other pets that have been outdoors can also be the source of garden pests. Other houseplants or plants given as gifts can also help spread pests and diseases. Avoid such problems by washing your hands and taking simple, pragmatic precautions.

Grow insect- and fungus-resistant plant varieties and keep the garden strong and healthy. Keep air well circulated and fresh. Keep humidity around 50 percent and maintain the temperature about 75° F during the day and about 10° to 15° cooler at night.

▲ Wash your hands to avoid transmitting insects and diseases from other plants.

▲ Keep all debris off the floor. Clean the garden area regularly.

◀ Dip tools in alcohol to disinfect.

◀ Keep garden room temperatures about 75° F during the day and no less than 55° F at night, for the best results.

▼ Monitoring the temperature, both day and night, will help you answer many questions.

% Relative Humidity

▲ Keep relative humidity about 50 percent and avoid dynamic fluctuations to prevent difficulties.

Misdiagnosed Disorders

Many indoor garden problems are misdiagnosed as a lack or excess of fertilizer. Often, disease and insects cause such problems. Other times, problems are caused by an imbalanced growing medium or water pH. A pH between 5.5 to 6.5, in hydroponics, will allow nutrients to be chemically available.

Temperature and humidity also influence growth. Keep them in the ideal range for the plants you are growing. Regularly monitor the temperature of the nutrient solution to ensure it stays below 60° F.

Excess sodium (more than 50 PPM) in the water supply restricts water and nutrients from being absorbed by the roots.

Once a plant shows symptoms, it has already undergone nutritional stress. It will take time to resume vigorous growth.

Do not confuse nutrient deficiencies or toxicities with insect and disease damage or poor cultural practices.

Damage from Cultural Practices are the Following:

◆ Lack of ventilation to the plant – slow growth and curled down leaves.

◆ Lack of light – slow spindly growth and stretching between internodes.

◆ Excessive humidity – slow growth and curled down leaves.

◆ Not enough humidity – seldom a problem, and much water use.

◆ Too high temperature – slow growth, and drooping leaves.

◆ Too low temperature – slow growth, purpling, and no flowers.

◆ Spray application damage – burned spots.

◆ Ozone damage – burned patches on leaves.

◆ Over-watering – wilting and slow growth.

◆ Under-watering – wilting and slow growth.

◆ Light burn – burned patches on leaves.

◆ Indoor air pollution – slow growth and sickly appearance.

Use Clean Water

Avoid most common ailments by keeping the temperature, humidity, and light at the proper levels. Use clean water, the proper complete nutrient solution, maintain EC and pH at the correct proportions, and change and flush the system with fresh nutrient solution every week.

▲ Circulate the air to avoid stratification.

▲ In-line vent fans move air quickly and quietly.

▶ Keep plenty of light on the garden, but do not keep lamps so close that they burn the foliage.

▲ Close up of a spider mite.

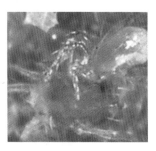

▲ Close up of a predatory mite
attacking a spider mite.

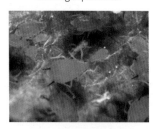

▲ Aphids are big enough to see
with the naked eye.

Spider Mites and Insects

Spider Mites

Spider mites are common indoors. Find spider mites on leaf undersides, sucking plant fluids. They look like tiny specks and cause yellowish-white spots on the tops of leaves. If infested, spider webs may be seen when misted with water. A magnifying glass (10-30X) helps to identify the yellow, white, two spotted, brown, or red mites and their translucent eggs.

Control of Spider Mites

- Clean up regularly.
- Raise humidity and temperature.
- Smear Tanglefoot™ around the pot lip and stems.
- Dip small plants and spray large ones with pyrethrum or neem oil.
- Introduce predatory mites.

Aphids

Aphids, about the size of a pinhead, are easy to see with the naked eye. With or without wings, they exude sticky honeydew that attracts ants that feed on it. If you see ants, look for aphids! Aphids suck plant sap and cause leaves to wilt and yellow.

Manually remove small numbers or spot spray small infestations with insecticidal soap. Control ants. Introduce lacewing or ladybug predators.

Whiteflies

Whiteflies flutter and fly from under leaves when disturbed. They look like a small, white moth about one millimeter long. Adults have wings. Eggs are also found on leaf undersides. Whiteflies cause whitish speckles, stipples, on the tops of leaves.

▲ Winged whiteflies on leaf underside.

Attract and kill adults with bright yellow, sticky traps that are placed among plants. The wasp, *Encarisa formosa,* is the most effective whitefly parasite. Kill with insecticidal soap or pyrethrum applied at 5 to10 day intervals.

Thrips

Tiny winged thrips are hard to see and easy to spot. Shake a branch and if white, gray, dark, or sometimes striped thrips are present, they will run. Thrips scrape plant tissue and suck juices, and whitish-yellow specks on top of leaves result. Leaves become brittle and dotted with feces. Thrips also wrap themselves in leaves and flowers.

▲ Translucent thrip nymph.

Control with predatory mites, parasitic wasps, pirate bugs, tobacco or nicotine-base sprays, pyrethrum, synthetic pyrethrum, or insecticidal soap.

Fungus Gnats

Larvae grow four to five millimeters long with translucent bodies and black heads. Winged adults are gray to black with long legs. Pests infest growing mediums and roots, eating and scaring roots. Plants loose vigor, foliage pales, and wounds invite disease.

▶ Dark specks are fungus gnats.

Control with Vectobac®, Gnatrol® and Bt-i. Use neem or insecticidal soap as a soil drench.

▲ 'Damping-off' rots seedlings and cuttings at the soil line.

▲ Green algae grow in light and nutrient-rich environments. Avoid algae by covering growing mediums.

Diseases

Gray Mold (Botrytis)

Gray mold flourishes in moist-temperate climates and is fatal. Botrytis appears hair-like, similar to laundry lint and later turns slimy, but can appear as dark, brownish spots on stems and flowers in arid climates. It attacks stems, leaves, seeds, and can cause damping-off.

Prevent gray mold by increasing air circulation and ventilation. Use fresh, clean growing medium. Remove infected foliage with alcohol-sterilized pruners and destroy. Wash your hands and tools.

Damping-off

Damping-off is fatal. It prevents sprouted seeds from emerging. Seedlings and cuttings rot at soil line. Foliage in older plants yellow and stems rot. First, the stem looses girth at the soil line, then grows dark, and finally falls over.

Avoid by controlling the growing medium moisture. Dust seeds with fungicide.

Green Algae

Slimy, green algae needs nutrients, light, and a moist surface to grow. Algae grows on moist rockwool and other moist-growing mediums exposed to light. They cause little damage, but attract fungus gnats, and other pests and diseases.

Cover moist-growing mediums to exclude light. Add an algaecide to the nutrient solution.

▲ Botrytis on plant stem.

Powdery Mildew

Small spots on the tops of leaves progresses to a fine, pale gray/white powdery coating on growing shoots, leaves, and stems. Growth slows, leaves yellow, and plants die as the disease advances.

Avoid cool, damp, humid, dim, and dirty conditions. Increase air circulation, ventilation, and light intensity. Avoid excess nitrogen. Control with Serenade®, or spray with a saturation-mix of baking soda and water.

Root Rot

Root rot turns roots dark brown, slows growth, leaves discolor, older foliage and later the entire plant wilts. Root rot is caused by lack of oxygen and soggy substrate.

Use fresh, sterile growing medium and keep the garden clean. Keep calcium levels adequate and avoid excess nitrogen. Keep pH above 6.0 in hydroponic units, and use Bio-Fungus® or RootShield®.

Fusarium Wilt and Verticillium Wilt

Wilt starts as small spots, soon older, lower leaves die. Leaf tips may curl before wilting and suddenly drying to a crisp. Portions of the plant, or the entire plant, wilts suddenly.

Keep garden clean and use fresh, clean growing medium. Avoid excess nitrogen.

Use Trichoderma against Fusarium and Bio-Fungus® on Verticillium. Treat seeds with fungicide before planting.

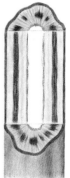

▶ Wilts affect the fluid flow, causing plants to wilt quickly. Cut the stem open on a severely affected plant. If a wilt is present, you will see the fluid transport system discolored and blocked.

▶ Powdery mildew grows in cool, moist environments.

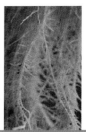

▶ Root rot causes roots to turn brown and slimy.

▲ Small hand-pump sprayers are convenient and economical.

▲ Larger pump-up sprayers are efficient for big gardens.

Controls and Spraying

Pests and diseases can often be avoided by making sure the garden area is clean. Inspect foliage and roots regularly for signs of pests and diseases. Control the growing environment to ensure plants are strong and healthy. Sometimes even with the best intentions, pests and diseases get a grip in the garden and must be removed.

Once you have determined you must spray, assess the damage and identify the pest or disease. Once identified, you can take cultural measures or purchase the proper product to rid the garden of the plague.

◆ Use only contact sprays approved for edible fruits and vegetables.

◆ Do not use TOXIC, SYSTEMIC CHEMICALS!

◆ Read the entire label on all sprays and follow directions.

◆ Mix pesticides and fungicides just before using.

◆ Safely dispose of unused sprays.

◆ Organic and natural-based sprays are also toxic and should be used sparingly.

◆ Spray both sides of leaves and stems.

◆ Rinse leaves on both sides with plain water 24 to 48 hours after spraying.

◆ Use protective gear, including a facemask when spraying, especially if using an aerosol/fogger.

◆ Raise lamps up and out of the way.

Metric Conversion Chart - Approximations

When You Know	Multiply by	To Find...
Length		
millimeters	0.04	inches
centimeters	0.39	inches
meters	3.28	feet
kilometers	0.62	miles
inches	25.40	millimeters
inches	2.54	centimeters
feet	30.48	centimeters
yards	0.91	meters
miles	1.16	kilometers
Area		
square centimeters	0.16	square inches
square meters	1.20	square yards
square kilometers	0.39	square miles
hectares	2.47	acres
square inches	6.45	square centimeters
square feet	0.09	square meters
square yards	0.84	square meters
square miles	2.60	square kilometers
acres	0.40	hectares
Volume		
milliliters	0.20	teaspoons
milliliters	0.60	tablespoons
milliliters	0.03	fluid ounces
liters	4.23	cups
liters	2.12	pints
liters	1.06	quarts
liters	0.26	gallons
cubic meters	35.32	cubic feet
cubic meters	1.35	cubic yards
teaspoons	4.93	milliliters
tablespoons	14.78	milliliters
fluid ounces	29.57	milliliters
cups	0.24	liters
pints	0.47	liters
quarts	0.95	liters
gallons	3.790	liters
Mass and Weight		
grams	0.035	ounce
kilogams	2.21	pounds
ounces	28.35	grams
pounds	0.45	kilograms

Equivalents

Length/Distance

1 inch (in.) = 25.4 millimeters (mm)
1 foot (12 in.) = 0.3048 meters (m)
1 yard (3 ft) = 0.9144 meters
1 mile = 1.60937 kilometers
1 millimeter = 0.03937014 inches (UK)
1 millimeter = 0.03937 inches (US)
1 centimeter = 0.3937014 inches (UK)
1 centimeter = 0.3937 inches (US)
1 meter = 3.280845 feet (UK)
1 meter = 3.280833 feet (US)
1 kilometer = 0.6213722 miles

Area

1 square inch = 645 square millimeters
1 square foot = 0.0929 square meters
1 square yard = 0.8361 square meters
1 square mile = 2.59 square kilometers

Liquid Measure Conversion

1 pint (UK) = 0.56824 liters
1 pint dry (US) = 0.55059 liters
1 pint liquid (US) = 0.47316 liters
1 gallon (UK) (8 pints) = 4.5459 liters
1 gallon dry (US) = 4.4047 liters
1 pint liquid (US) = 3.7853 liters

Weight

1 ounce = 28.3495 grams
1 pound (16 ounces) = 0.453592 kilograms
1 gram = 15.4325 grains
1 kilogram = 2.2046223 pounds

Celsius to Fahrenheit

Degrees Celsius = (degrees Fahrenheit - 32) x 5/9
Degrees Fahrenheit = (degrees Celsius x 9/5) +32

Light Conversion

1 foot-candle = 10.76 = lux
1 lux = 0.09293
Lux = 1 lumen/square meters